Juneteenth

Denise M. Jordan

Heinemann Library
Chicago, Illinois

© 2003 Heinemann Library
a division of Reed Elsevier Inc.
Chicago, Illinois

Customer Service 888–454–2279
Visit our website at www.heinemannlibrary.com

Page layout by Jennifer Lee
Printed and bound in China by South China Printing Company

07 06 05
10 9 8 7 6 5 4 3 2

Library of Congress Cataloging-in-Publication Data
Jordan, Denise.
    Juneteenth / Denise M. Jordan.
        p. cm. -- (Holiday histories)
Summary: Describes the holiday known as Juneteenth Day, which has roots in Texas and which celebrates the end of slavery in the United States.
Includes bibliographical references (p.) and index.
    ISBN 1-4034-3505-7 (HC), 1-4034-3690-8 (pbk.)
    1. Juneteenth--Juvenile literature. 2.
Slaves--Emancipation--Texas--Juvenile literature. 3. African Americans--Texas--Galveston--History--Juvenile literature. 4. African Americans--Anniversaries, etc.--Juvenile literature. 5. African Americans--Social life and customs--Juvenile literature. 6. Slaves--Emancipation--United States--Juvenile literature. [1. Juneteenth. 2. Slaves--Emancipation. 3. Holidays.] I. Title. II. Series.

E185.93.T4J67 2003

394.263--dc21

Acknowledgments
The author and publishers are grateful to the following for permission to reproduce copyright material:

Cover photograph by Dwayne Newton/PhotoEdit

p. 5 Michael Keller/Corbis; pp. 6, 7, 11, 12, 15, 18 Bettmann/Corbis; pp. 8, 9, 10, 13, 26 Corbis; pp. 14, 21, 22, 23 Hulton Archive/Getty Images; pp. 16-17 Library of Congress; pp. 19, 20 The Granger Collection, N.Y; p. 24 Robert Brenner/PhotoEdit; p. 25 Tom Carter/PhotoEdit; p. 27 Joe Harpring/AP Wide World Photo; p. 28 Joseph Sohm/ChromoSohm Inc./Corbis; p. 29 Dwayne Newton/PhotoEdit

Photo research by Kathy Creech

Every effort has been made to contact copyright holders of any material reproduced in this book. Any omissions will be rectified in subsequent printings if notice is given to the publisher.

Some words are shown in bold, **like this.** You can find out what they mean by looking in the glossary.

Contents

A Celebration of Freedom

The smell of barbecue is strong in the air. Food covers the picnic tables. Families gather together to celebrate the day of freedom.

Children listen as their elders tell the story of freedom. History is being celebrated. What day is it? It's Juneteenth Day!

Many slaves were forced to work in cotton fields.

What Is Juneteenth Day?

Juneteenth Day is the oldest African-American holiday. It was the very last day of **slavery** in the United States. It was the day all **slaves** learned they were free.

This painting shows Abraham Lincoln reading the
Emancipation Proclamation.

Abraham Lincoln was the President of the
United States. He ordered all slaves to be
freed on January 1, 1863. Slaves in most
states heard the news. But the slaves in
Texas were not told. They were told on
June 19, 1865.

Why Were African - Americans Slaves?

Many southern states had large farms called **plantations.** The owners of the large farms needed a lot of workers. They wanted workers they did not have to pay.

*This drawing show **slaves** being sold. Many families were separated when they were sold to different owners.*

Men hired ships and sailed to Africa.
They trapped African men, women,
and children to take back to America.
The Africans were then sold into **slavery.**

An Argument Over Slavery

*Fredrick Douglass escaped slavery. He became an **abolitionist** and a writer.*

Some people believed that **slavery** was wrong. Many northern leaders wanted to end slavery. But **plantation** owners did not want to free the **slaves.**

These men are having a meeting about slavery. Many people wanted to end slavery.

Southern leaders were tired of the northern leaders telling them to free the slaves. They decided to form their own government.

★

A War Is Started

President Abraham Lincoln said the southern states could not form their own government. If they tried, he would send the army to stop them.

These men were part of the Confederate States of America.

The southern states started their own government. They called themselves the Confederate States of America. They formed an army and navy. Then, they attacked the United States and started the **Civil War.**

★
13

Rumors of Freedom

During the **Civil War,** Lincoln put out an order freeing all **slaves.** It was called the **Emancipation Proclamation.** Most slave owners refused to tell their slaves about freedom. But **rumors** of freedom quickly spread throughout the South.

During the Civil War the states that stayed loyal to the government were known as the Union. This Union soldier is removing the chains from a slave.

One person told another, then another, then another. Just by word of mouth slaves learned the news. Some slaves left the **plantations** and headed for the city. Some of them went to help the Union soldiers.

★

The Union Goes to Texas

Slaves in Texas were not told about freedom. The **plantation** owners did not want to lose their slaves. If slaves talked about freedom they were punished.

*During the Civil War many **freed** slaves joined the Union army.*

On April 9, 1865 the Confederate army
surrendered. The **Civil War** was over.
The Union troops marched into Texas and
brought news of freedom.

Free at Last

This drawing is showing a family of slaves receiving the news of freedom.

On June 19, 1865, Union General Gordon Granger went to Galveston, Texas. He read an order that stated "all **slaves** are free." The news spread quickly.

Some slaves shouted for joy. Others hugged
family members, cried silently, or prayed.
Many began to celebrate. The long wait
was over.

Celebrating Freedom

People everywhere celebrated the end of **slavery.** They brought food and drinks to share. They danced and sang. Children played games.

African-Americans no longer had to fear being sold into slavery. They were no longer forced to work for free. They were no longer considered to be another man's property. They were finally free.

Why Is Juneteenth Day Called Juneteenth Day?

These children were allowed to learn how to read and write.

In the South, only white children were allowed to go to school. It was against the law to teach **slaves** how to read and write. Some slave owners would punish their slaves if they found out that the slaves could read.

These children were slaves. It was against the law for them to learn how to read and write.

Since slaves were not allowed to go to school they pronounced some words differently. During all the telling and retelling of the last days of **slavery,** June 19 became Juneteenth.

How Is Juneteenth Celebrated Today?

Many cities like Houston, Dallas, and Fort Worth, Texas, hold big parades. People cheer as colorful floats, marching bands, and community groups go by.

Besides games and food, storytelling is a part of the celebration. Stories are told to remind people about the first days of freedom.

Where Are Juneteenth Celebrations Held?

Early Juneteenth celebrations were held at churches. Some were held in fields in the country. Later, **freed slaves** purchased a park to have Juneteenth celebrations.

Today, Juneteenth celebrations are held in schools, churches, community centers, and city parks. Many people even have small Juneteenth celebrations in their homes.

Juneteenth Jubilee

Most people celebrate Juneteenth Day on June 19. Some celebrate on January 1, the day Lincoln ordered **slaves** to be **freed.** Others celebrate on the day slaves were freed in their state.

Juneteenth Day is not a national holiday. Only eight states have made it a state holiday – Texas, Florida, Oklahoma, Delaware, Alaska, Idaho, Iowa, and California. However, Juneteenth Day is celebrated in many states across the country.

★

Important Dates

Juneteenth

1860	Abraham Lincoln is elected president of the United States.
1861	The Civil War begins when the Confederacy fires cannons at Fort Sumter.
1863	President Lincoln issues the **Emancipation Proclamation.**
1865	The Confederacy **surrenders** on April 9, 1865; the Civil War ends.
1865	June 19. General Granger reads General Orders Number 3 informing Texas **slaves** of their freedom. This is the last day of **slavery** in the United States.
1866	The first Juneteenth Day is celebrated in Texas.
1872	Emancipation Park purchased by **freed** slaves in Houston, Texas to hold Juneteenth celebrations.
1892	Booker T. Washington Park, near Mexia, Texas, purchased by freed slaves to hold Juneteenth celebrations.
1980	Texas makes Juneteenth Day a state holiday.
1994	Movement started to make Juneteenth Day a national holiday.

Glossary

abolitionist a person who speaks out against slavery.

Civil War the war between the southern and northern states of the United States.

Emancipation Proclamation a statement signed by President Abraham Lincoln freeing slaves.

freed not controlled by someone else.

planation a large farm where crops such as coffee, sugar, or cotton are grown.

rumor a story that is passed along from person to person.

slave person who works for someone else for no money.

slavery the practice of owning slaves.

surrender to give up.

More Books to Read

Branch, Muriel Miller. *Juneteenth: Freedom day*. New York: Cobblehill Books, 1998.

Taylor, Charles A. *Juneteenth A Celebration of Freedom*. Greensboro: Open Hand Publishing, LLC, 2002.

Weatherford, Carole Boston. *Juneteenth Jamboree*. New York: Lee & Low Books, 1998.

Index